Mexican AMERICANS

Our CULTURAL HERITAGE

SPIRIT
of America®

Mexican Americans

By Judy Alter

The Child's World®
Chanhassen, Minnesota

6

Mexican AMERICANS

Published in the United States of America by The Child's World®
PO Box 326 • Chanhassen, MN 55317-0326 • 800-599-READ • www.childsworld.com

Acknowledgments
The Child's World®: Mary Berendes, Publishing Director

Editorial Directions, Inc.: E. Russell Primm, Emily Dolbear, Sarah E. De Capua, and Lucia Raatma, Editors; Linda S. Koutris, Photo Selector; Image Select International, Photo Research; Red Line Editorial and Pam Rosenberg, Fact Research; Tim Griffin/IndexServ, Indexer; Chad Rubel, Proofreader

Photos
Cover/frontispiece: A Mexican-American family in San Antonio, Texas, 1939

Cover photographs ©: Library of Congress; Digital Vision, Inc.

Interior photographs ©: Getty Images, 6; Corbis, 7 top; AKG-images, Berlin, 7 bottom; Corbis, 9 top; AKG-images, Berlin, 9 bottom, 10; Corbis, 11; TRIP/S.Grant, 12; Corbis, 13; Getty Images, 14, 15; TRIP/S. Grant, 16; TRIP/ASK Images, 17; TRIP/G. Dowen, 18; AFP, 19 top; Digitalvision, 19 bottom; Topham, 20; Getty Images, 21; Topham 22, TRIP/S. Grant, 23; Corbis, 24, 25 top, 25 bottom; Getty Images, 26; Corbis, 27, 28.

Library of Congress Cataloging-in-Publication Data
Alter, Judy, 1938–
Mexican Americans / by Judy Alter.
    p. cm.
Summary: Introduces the customs, heritage, and traditions of Mexican Americans.
Includes index.
ISBN 1-56766-156-4 (Library Bound : alk. paper)
1. Mexican Americans—Juvenile literature. [1. Mexican Americans.] I.Title.
E184.M5 A66 2002
973'.046872—dc21
                        2001007820

13   21   24

Contents

Chapter ONE

The First Mexican Americans

MEXICO IS THE ONLY COUNTRY WHOSE BORDER touches the mainland United States to the south. It is the third-largest country in North America after Canada and the United States. In the first half of the 19th century, Mexico owned and controlled much of the present southwestern United States. Many Mexicans lived north of the Rio Grande, mainly in New Mexico and

American troops attacking Mexico City during the Mexican-American War

California. Today many Mexican Americans are not **immigrants** but **descendants** of people who lived in U.S. territory when the land belonged to Mexico. The Texas Revolution (1835–1836) and the Mexican-American War (1846–1848) established the present boundaries

A family living in a jacal on the U.S.-Mexican border near the Rio Grande

between the two countries. At that time, some 75,000 Mexicans found themselves living in America rather than Mexico. Most of them stayed in America and became the first Mexican-American citizens.

Mexico has historically been a poor, **rural** country. Farmers tried to raise squash, beans, and maize, or corn, on small patches of land. Most Mexicans lived in small villages. Their houses, called *jacals* (ha-KALS), were log or **adobe** huts with mud floors and roofs made of grass or palm leaves. Women cooked over open fires. Families often slept on mats on the ground. Even today, many

The violence of the Mexican Revolution led a large number of Mexicans to leave their country.

▶ American cowboys owe their language, dress, and work habits to the Mexican *vaqueros* (va-KAYR-ohs) who worked in California in the early 19th century. Vaqueros were horsemen who handled large herds of cattle on the open range. They wore heavy leather trousers called *chaparreras* (chah-pah-RRAYR-ahs) to protect their legs from thorny bushes. The chaparreras became the cowboys' chaps. Vaqueros wore wide-brimmed hats to protect them from the elements. Cowboys' Stetson hats are based on those vaqueros' hats. Vaqueros called the annual roundup a *rodeo*.

farmers have no modern tools or equipment. Droughts are frequent, and life is hard.

Until the early 20th century, these people came to the United States in small numbers. The bloody Mexican Revolution (1910–1917) drove more Mexicans to seek safety north of the border. At that time, the United States allowed unlimited immigration. Most Mexican immigrants were poor and uneducated. They worked on railroads or in mining and **agriculture**. A few had skills as carpenters, blacksmiths, barbers, and shoemakers.

During World War I (1914–1918), American factories needed workers to replace the men who had gone to war. Mexicans then began to get better jobs at higher wages. They began to move to midwestern and northern cities. For example, many worked in the automobile factories in Detroit, Michigan. In the 1930s, the Great Depression brought unemployment to the United States. American citizens resented Mexican Americans who took jobs that citizens wanted. Many immigrants returned to Mexico. During World War II (1939–1945), the United States again wanted Mexican-American workers. The government started the *bracero* (hired hand) program and issued temporary **visas** to Mexican workers. Employers often took advantage of braceros, forcing Mexicans to work long hours for low pay and to live in poor conditions.

A Mexican family coming to America as part of the bracero program

Until the 1950s, most Mexicans came to America as **migrant workers**. They did not want to leave their homes in Mexico, but better jobs were available in the United States. Men came alone and worked during the harvest season. They sent money home to their families. After the harvest, they returned to Mexico. Some came legally, with visas that allowed them to work. However, many others crossed the border and entered the United States without the permission of the U.S. government.

Border patrol officers at the U.S.-Mexico border noting footprints of illegal immigrants in the sand

UNTIL THE 16TH century, various Indian tribes ruled Mexico. The Maya civilization developed great cities, pyramids, and a written language as early as 300 B.C. By the 16th century, the Aztec people dominated much of Mexico.

In the 1500s, Spain defeated the Aztecs (above) and took control of Mexico and its various Indian tribes. The Spanish introduced Roman Catholicism to Mexico. They sent conquistadors, or leaders in the conquest of Mexico, north across the Rio Grande to look for gold. Much of what is now the southwestern United States was then part of Mexico. Many Mexicans today are descendants of both native Indian people and the Spanish.

In 1821, Mexico won its independence from Spain. In 1836, Mexican troops under General Antonio López de Santa Anna (below) massacred about 200 Texans—Americans living in Texas—at the Battle of the Alamo in San Antonio de Bexar (present-day San Antonio). That same year, the Mexican army was driven from Texas after Texans defeated Santa Anna and his troops at the Battle of San Jacinto. Texas was no longer a part of Mexico.

Mexico still controlled much of the Southwest, however, from New Mexico to California. The Mexican-American War, fought from 1846 to 1848, ended with the Treaty of Guadalupe Hidalgo, which established most of the present boundaries. In 1854, the United States

completed the purchase of a small strip of land near the Rio Grande from Mexico. Known as the Gadsden Purchase, this transaction completed the establishment of the boundaries between the two countries.

Chapter Two

Mexicans in the United States

As the years have passed, Mexican Americans have begun to work in a variety of professions.

MANY MEXICAN IMMIGRANTS ARE FARMERS and laborers. Professional people such as lawyers and doctors also come to the United States hoping to find a better life. However, some do not have enough training to practice their profession in this country. Strict laws govern the amount of education and training required to be a doctor, lawyer, or other professional in the United States. As a result, some immigrants must take other jobs. But many Americans continue to believe that all Mexican immigrants are poor, uneducated **peasants**.

Mexicans have not always received a warm welcome in the

United States. When the United States received land from Mexico in 1848, after the Mexican-American War, the U.S. government promised Mexicans living on that land that they could keep their property. In spite of this, **Anglo** settlers took the Mexicans' land. These Anglo settlers wanted to control the Southwest. They wanted to make the towns more American and stamp out all evidence of

A Mexican tortilla maker demonstrating his craft during a California fiesta

Mexican **culture**. Towns passed laws outlawing fiestas, or celebrations. Restaurants and stores did not allow Mexicans to enter. Mexicans were refused jobs. They were not allowed to bury their dead in local cemeteries. Mexicans were labeled as poor and lazy. Many Mexicans did not speak English, which made daily life even harder for them. As a result, some returned to Mexico.

13

Cesar Chavez was an important spokesman for the Chicano people.

Those who stayed in the United States tried to think of themselves as American citizens. Between 350,000 and 500,000 Mexican Americans fought for the United States in World War II (1939–1945). They earned 39 Congressional Medals of Honor—the highest military awards. Members of the armed forces earn these honors for showing extraordinary bravery during battle. Under the **GI Bill**, many servicemen went back to school and earned college degrees. The GI Bill was passed by the U.S. Congress to give better opportunities to GIs who had served their country. They were trained for better jobs, but many still faced **discrimination**. Some became **activists** for the advancement of Mexican Americans.

Cesar Chavez (1927–1993) was the most famous Mexican-American activist. In the

1950s, he began organizing grape pickers in California. Chavez told the world how poorly undocumented workers were being treated. He led the workers in strikes. In the 1960s, the **Chicano** movement—El Movimiento—developed, inspired both by Chavez's work and the black civil rights movement. The movement fought for equal rights, pay, and recognition for Mexican Americans. The term Chicano, once considered insulting, became a symbol of ethnic pride.

Mexican neighborhoods, like this one in Queens, New York, can be found throughout the United States.

Some immigrants arrived in America dreaming of a house in the **suburbs** and a fine education for their children. Instead, many Mexicans found themselves living in communities called barrios. Although the word barrio means "neighborhood," it came to mean "ghetto" because barrios were generally in poor districts. Newcomers

were welcomed and helped to find work by relatives and friends in these communities. In the barrios, Mexicans preserved their

15

traditional ways. They spoke Spanish, and they shopped at stores that carried Mexican foods.

Mexicans place great value on the family as a source of strength. Family includes grandparents and aunts and uncles and cousins, who often live together in the same home. Having respect for elders is a part of this family-oriented tradition. Through most of the 20th century, elders were obeyed without question. Marriages were arranged, and daughters obeyed. Jobs were suggested, and sons obeyed.

The family remains a vital part of Mexican-American life.

Mexican culture is traditionally dominated by males. The man was the *jefe de la casa*, or "the chief of the household" and his word was law. In the past, even in America, the life choices of most Mexican women were limited to marriage, entering a **convent** as a nun, or taking care of elderly parents. Until the late 20th century, Mexican Americans generally followed the lifestyles established by their families in Mexico.

ILLEGAL IMMIGRANTS FROM MEXICO became a major problem for the United States in the 1960s. Mexicans who do not qualify for immigration come secretly into the country, often by swimming across the Rio Grande.

Illegal entrants are called "undocumented workers." They do not have a visa—a government permit to enter the country. Temporary nonimmigrant visas are issued to people coming to the United States temporarily. Immigrants who have jobs or relatives in the United States are given permanent visas. There is a long waiting list for visas, and the process of getting one is complicated.

To work in America legally, an immigrant must have a visa and a green card—a document that makes him or her a resident of the United States. U.S. government agencies sometimes visit businesses looking for Mexican workers without green cards. This happens most often in the Southwest.

About 4 million undocumented workers come into the United States every year. Of the 1 million who are caught and sent back to Mexico, most try to reenter the United States. Sometimes Mexican citizens pay a coyote, or smuggler, to help them enter the United States illegally.

Chapter THREE

Keeping Traditions

Many residents of Mexico live in poor conditions and hope to make a better life in America.

MEXICO TODAY IS THE LARGEST SPANISH-speaking country in the world. It has more than 100 million residents. However, the Mexican economy is still extremely poor. Americans own eight times as many cars as Mexicans. They have ten times as many telephones and five times as many televisions. They spend eight times as much educating their children. Some Americans earn 20 times what a Mexican earns in a similar job. Mexicans come to America hoping to share in this wealth.

More than 20 million Mexicans live in the United States today. Most have settled in New Mexico and California,

but large Mexican-American communities are also found in Arizona, Colorado, Florida, Illinois, Nevada, New Jersey, New York, and Texas. Mexicans are close to overtaking African-Americans as the largest minority in America.

A Virgin of Guadalupe festival in a Mexican-American section of Los Angeles

More than immigrants from many other countries, Mexican Americans have kept their native culture. They continue to speak Spanish, eat traditional foods, and live together. In most cases, they continue to practice Roman Catholicism, the religion of their homeland. Many homes today contain statues of the Virgin Mary or, as she is called in the Southwest, the Virgin of Guadalupe.

Traditional Mexican food can include tortilla chips, beans, tomatoes, limes, and avocados.

Some traditional Mexican ways are changing, though, in Mexican-American culture. Machismo—an exaggerated

A Mexican-American first-grader enjoying a bilingual music class in California

sense of male superiority—is not as popular as it used to be. Mexican-American women, called Chicanas, are moving into business, political, and social roles. In the past, Mexican men came to this country alone and sent money to their families back home. Today, they bring their families. The elderly are no longer obeyed without question. While most Mexican young people still respect their elders, they are inclined to make lifestyle decisions for themselves.

Mexican Americans have the next-to-lowest record of educational achievement of any minority population in the United States. Only Native Americans have a worse record. Most Mexican Americans born in this country graduate from high school, but immigrants who arrive as teenagers rarely graduate. Only a small percentage of Mexican-American high-school graduates go on to college. Of those, an even smaller number actually earn degrees. Those who complete their education, however, can achieve great success. Mexican Americans are increasingly represented in law, medicine, teaching, financial occupations, and government jobs. With this success, Mexican Americans have moved from the barrios to the suburbs.

Mexican Americans do not have the political power one might expect of so large a population, however. Many have not met the requirements for citizenship. A person must speak English and understand the American government to become a U.S. citizen. Those who have become U.S. citizens frequently exercise their right to vote, which comes with citizenship. As more Mexican Americans vote, Mexican-American candidates get elected to political offices throughout the country. One of the first Mexican Americans to reach high political office was Henry Cisneros. He was the first Mexican-American mayor of San Antonio, Texas, serving from 1981 to 1989. He then served as the secretary of the Department of Housing and Urban Development from 1993 to 1997 under President Bill Clinton.

Henry Cisneros, one of the most successful Mexican-American politicians

MOST MEXICAN-AMERICAN PEOPLE SPEAK SPANISH AT HOME. PEOPLE in Mexican-American communities shop at stores where Spanish is spoken; they listen to Mexican-American radio stations; and they watch television channels with Spanish programming. Many public signs (below) and advertisements are now printed in both English and Spanish.

Children from Spanish-speaking households are at a disadvantage in school. Because they cannot understand lessons given in English, they cannot do the required schoolwork. Mexican-American students who do not get a good education continue to live in poverty—the very situation that their families tried to escape from.

Bilingual education teaches students the basic subjects, including reading and writing, in their native language. But students also begin learning English from the first day in school.

People who do not support bilingual education say it is too expensive to hire qualified teachers and buy the needed books and materials. They argue that research shows that many Mexican Americans have achieved success without bilingual education. They believe that being allowed to rely on Spanish often delays children's progress in their English-based education. Some also insist that if people want to live in the United States, they should learn the language of the land.

Chapter FOUR

Mexican-American Contributions

MEXICANS HAVE ENRICHED AMERICAN LIVES with their traditions. For example, their culture has dramatically changed American eating habits. The basic ingredients of Mexican cooking are corn, rice, beans, meat, and a variety of chili peppers. Many chain and fast-food restaurants throughout the United States serve Mexican food. Much of it is really "Tex-Mex," a blend of Mexican and Texan cooking traditions. Foods such as tacos, enchiladas, burritos, and chili rely on chili powder and jalapeño peppers for their "Mexican" flavor.

Tacos, burritos, and other Tex-Mex foods

A woman chopping cilantro, a key ingredient in traditional Mexican cooking

Traditional Mexican cooking mixes Spanish and Indian flavors. It relies on cilantro, tomatillos, Mexican cheeses, and spices such as cumin. *Pollo mole* (POH-yoh MOH-lay) is a traditional chicken dish in which the sauce has a hint of chocolate. *Carne adovada* (KAR-nay ah-doh-VAH-dah) is a spicy pork stew made with several kinds of chilis. There are many more *sopas* (soups) than the tortilla soup found on the menu of countless restaurants. Tamales were first made centuries ago by Mexican Indians, the earliest inhabitants of Mexico.

Mexicans have also made rich contributions to the language of Americans. The word "rodeo" comes from the Spanish words *rodear* (to surround) and *rueda* (wheel). Other words such as bonanza, fiesta,

The word rodeo, now used for an American pastime, originated in the Spanish language

Folksinger Joan Baez

mesa, canyon, and coyote are Spanish, too. Spanish place names in the United States include San Antonio and El Paso (Texas), San Diego and Los Angeles (California), and Colorado.

Mexican contributions in music, art, and literature are less well known to most Americans. Much Mexican music is folk music. In the Southwest, Mexican Americans still sing *corridos*— folk ballads that tell the story of heroes and outlaws and even of labor reformer Cesar Chavez. In Texas, a brand of music known as Tex-Mex developed when Mexican Americans blended their guitars and banjos with the accordions and folk music of German Texans. Originally instrumental music, Tex-Mex now includes lyrics about the Mexican-American experience. Many Mexican restaurants in the United States feature mariachi bands. Joan Baez, who came to fame during the Chicano movement, is a Mexican entertainer with a national reputation as a folksinger.

Since the Chicano movement, Mexican authors and artists have received increased attention. Chicano literature stresses the themes of land and family. A few Mexican-American writers have gained national prominence. One of them is Rudolfo Anaya. His novel, *Bless Me, Ultima,* tells of a young Mexican-American boy learning to understand his mixed heritage. Another author is Sandra Cisneros. Her short-story collection, *The House on Mango Street*, was first issued by a small press that published Mexican writing. A major New York publisher later reprinted it, giving more Americans an opportunity to read it.

Mexican-American artists are also receiving significant recognition. Their work is heavily influenced by the Spanish Catholic heritage and also by the art of Mexican-Indian cultures. Powerful murals, or wall paintings, portray the lives of Mexican migrant workers, and artists still carve *santos*, figures representing saints.

Much Southwestern architecture shows Mexican influence. Homes, churches, and public buildings may

Mexican murals in a Chicago neighborhood

27

be made of adobe with tile floors and traditional logs in the ceiling. Houses may be decorated in the Mexican style with rugs, blankets, and vases.

All these influences are strongest in the American Southwest. But Mexican culture has changed life throughout the entire United States. Mexican Americans have developed a sense of pride in their place in America. There are still quarrels about the employment of Mexicans living illegally in the United States, bilingual education, and other issues.

Many homes throughout the United States are decorated with Mexican rugs and art.

But Mexican Americans are an important and growing part of the United States population.

300 B.C. The Mayas rule Mexico.

1500s A.D. Spanish conquistadors defeat the Aztecs.

1821 Mexico wins its independence from Spain.

1835 The Texas Revolution begins.

1836 Santa Anna's troops defeat the Texans at the Alamo. Shortly after, the Texans defeat Santa Anna and end the Texas Revolution.

1846–1848 The Mexican-American War rages.

1848 Many Mexicans find themselves living in the United States after the Treaty of Guadalupe Hidalgo is signed.

1854 The Gadsden Purchase sets the boundary between the United States and Mexico.

1862 Mexico defeats French invaders. The day is referred to as "Cinco de Mayo" and is celebrated for years to come.

1910–1917 The Mexican Revolution ends with a new constitution for Mexico.

1914–1918 World War I erupts.

1930s The Great Depression puts many Americans out of work.

1939–1945 World War II leaves Europe in ruins. Mexican Americans earn 39 Congressional Medals of Honor.

1950s More Mexican migrant workers arrive in the United States.

1954–1958 The U.S. government creates a new deportation program, allowing officials to stop anyone who "looks Mexican" and request proof of American citizenship. While this policy is in effect, 3.8 million people of Hispanic origin leave the country.

1960s Illegal Mexican immigration becomes a serious problem in the United States. The Chicano movement begins.

1981 Henry Cisneros becomes the first Mexican-American mayor of San Antonio and eventually goes on to work in the Clinton administration. He is one of the first Mexican Americans to be elected to a high political office.

1982 The U.S. Supreme Court declares that children of immigrants without written proof of citizenship are entitled to the same public education as any other Americans.

1990s Illegal Mexican immigration continues to be a challenge for the United States. The benefits of bilingual education programs begin to be debated.

activists (AK-tiv-ists)
An activist is a person who speaks and acts on one side of an issue that people disagree about. Cesar Chavez was a famous Mexican-American activist.

adobe (uh-DOH-bee)
An adobe brick is made of clay mixed with straw and dried in the sun.

agriculture (AG-ri-kull-chur)
Agriculture is farming. Most Mexican immigrants in the early 20th century worked in agriculture.

Anglo (ANG-glow)
An Anglo is a white inhabitant of the United States who is not of Hispanic descent. Anglo settlers took Mexican land after the Mexican-American War.

Chicano (chi-KAHN-oh)
A Chicano is a male American of Mexican descent. A Chicana is an American female of Mexican descent.

convent (KAHN-vent)
A convent is a building where nuns live and worship.

culture (KULL-chur)
Culture includes the way of life, ideas, customs, and traditions of a group of people.

descendants (deh-SEN-dents)
Descendants are the family members of people who lived long ago.

discrimination (dis-krim-ih-NAY-shun)
Discrimination is treating others unfairly based on differences in age, race, or gender. Mexican Americans have often faced discrimination.

GI Bill (JEE EYE BILL)
The GI Bill was signed in 1944. It provided help in areas such as housing and education to people who served in the armed forces.

immigrants (IM-ih-grents)
An immigrant is someone who comes from one country to settle in another country. Many Americans have relatives who were immigrants.

luminaries (LOOM-in-air-eez)
Luminaries are decorative candleholders. Luminaries are often used to light doorways and walkways.

migrant workers (MY-grent WURK-erz)
Migrant workers move from place to place to find work, often as harvesters. Most Mexican immigrants, up until the 1950s, were migrant workers.

peasants (PEZ-ents)
A peasant owns or works on a small farm.

rural (RUR-ull)
Rural is related to the countryside or farming. Mexico has historically been a rural country.

suburbs (SUB-uhrbs)
Suburbs are areas at the outer edge of a city. A suburb is made up mostly of houses.

visas (VEE-suhz)
A visa is a document giving someone permission to enter a foreign country. Following World War II, the U.S. government issued temporary visas to Mexican workers in the bracero program.

Web Sites

Visit our homepage for lots of links about Mexican Americans:
http://www.childsworld.com/links.html

Note to Parents, Teachers, and Librarians:
We routinely verify our Web links to make sure they're safe,
active sites—so encourage your readers to check them out!

Books

Bunting, Eve. *A Day's Work.* Boston: Houghton Mifflin, 1994.

Garza, Carmen Lomas. *Magic Windows/Ventanas Magicas.* San Francisco: Children's Book Press, 1999.

Hoyt-Goldsmith, Diane. *Day of the Dead: A Mexican-American Celebration.* New York: Holiday House, 1994.

Levy, Janice. *Abuelito Eats with His Fingers.* Austin, Tex.: Eakin Publications, 1999.

Rodriguez, Luis J. *America Is Her Name.* Willimantic, Conn.: Curbstone Press, 1998.

Stanek, Muriel. *I Speak English for My Mom.* Skokie, Ill.: Albert Whitman, 1989.

Places to Visit or Contact

Mexican American Cultural Center
1001 Connecticut Avenue, N.W.
Suite 601
Washington, DC 20036
202-223-5500

Mexican Fine Arts Center Museum
1852 West 19th Street
Chicago, IL 60608
312-738-1503

The Mexican Museum
Fort Mason Center, Building D
San Francisco, CA 94123
415-441-0404

Index